CHESS MADE EASY

C.J.S. Purdy, A.M., (1906–79) was an International Chess Master. He was also World Correspondence Chess Champion, 1953–8, Champion of Australia, 1935–8 and 1949–52, Champion of New Zealand, 1925, and Champion of Australasia and S.E. Asia, 1960–3.

G. Koshnitsky, M.B.E., was born in Russia in 1907 and migrated to Australia in 1926. He is an International Master in Correspondence Chess and was Champion of Australia, 1933–4 and 1939–45. He was the Captain of the Australian Olympiad Chess Teams in 1964, 1968, 1972 and 1980.

D1328924

CHESS MADE EASY

C. J. S. Purdy, A.M.,
and G. Koshnitsky, M.B.E.

CLAREMONT BOOKS

PENGUIN BOOKS

Published by the Penguin Group
Penguin Books Ltd, 27 Wrights Lane, London W8 5TZ, England
Penguin Books USA Inc., 375 Hudson Street, New York, New York 10014, USA
Penguin Books Australia Ltd, Ringwood, Victoria, Australia
Penguin Books Canada Ltd, 10 Alcorn Avenue, Toronto, Ontario, Canada M4V 3B2
Penguin Books (NZ) Ltd, 182–190 Wairau Road, Auckland 10, New Zealand

Penguin Books Ltd, Registered Offices: Harmondsworth, Middlesex, England

First published by Chess World, 1942
26th Edition revised and updated

Published with minor revisions in Penguin Books 1994

This edition published by Claremont Books,
an imprint of Godfrey Cave Associates Limited,
42 Bloomsbury Street, London WC1B 3QJ,
under licence from Penguin Books Ltd, 1995

ISBN 1 85471 764 2

CONTENTS

INTRODUCTION

To die without having learnt chess is like dying without ever having heard music!

And chess is easy! That is, easy to learn to play well enough to enjoy it. Treated as a pastime, chess gives lasting pleasure because of its unending variety; you never tire of chess. But chess can be more to you than a game. 'Chess is an art, chess is a study, chess is one of the noblest inventions of the human mind,' said the philosopher C.E.M. Joad. Chess helps to mould character for it teaches equanimity in the face of good or ill fortune.

Many think that to play chess well one must memorise numerous openings. This is wrong. An understanding of general principles will suffice to attain average skill.

There is no 'chess type'. Chess appeals to diverse minds, for it is a blend of opposites. It is logical, yet quaint and picturesque. Some of its principles apply to modern war, yet it is redolent of ancient chivalry and romance. It combines the zest of struggle with rest from all cares. East and West meet in chess.

A thousand years ago chess was already the world's most widely played game, and it still is today.

Countless books have been written on chess. It has been a recreation of many of the world's famous people: Charlemagne, King Canute, Sir Walter Raleigh, Shakespeare, Ben Jonson, Leibnitz, Voltaire, Rousseau, Peter the Great, Frederick the Great, Napoleon, Buckle (the historian), Benjamin Franklin, Dickens, Ruskin, R.L. Stevenson, Lenin, Bonar Law, Fritz Kreisler, H.G. Wells – and too many contemporaries to mention.

THE GAME

Chess is a war game, perhaps dating back as much as fourteen centuries. Chess played on a board of 64 squares originated in Ancient India. The pieces then represented the four main parts of an army (infantry, cavalry, elephants and war chariots) plus the king and his counsellor.

Chess may have been a Buddhist invention, designed as a bloodless substitute for war. Anyway, an early Indian writer remarked after a long era of peace, 'Armies are now seen in action only on chessboards'.

Today, the quaint jumble of names that various languages (including English) give the chessmen smack of the paradoxical, fairy-tale world of Lewis Carroll, rather than of the grim realities of total war. All over the world, people like chess that way, and ignore attempts to modernise the names.

In English the elephants have become bishops. The cavalry, carved like horses' heads, have their medieval name, knights. The pieces in the corners were the war chariots: these are carved as towers, and were long called castles, but now are 'rooks'. Rook is a corruption of the Persian *rukh*, meaning a war chariot. The counsellor is now a queen.

OBJECT

Every unit, with one exception, is subject to capture by any opposing unit. That exception is the King, who is exempt from this indignity.

Yet the object of the game is the virtual capture of the King. This is called checkmate (in Persian *shahmat*, the King's death), universally abbreviated to 'mate'.

You will find this paradox resolved on p. 11, under the heading 'Check and Mate'. Check is a threat to capture the King, and mate is a check from which there is no escape.

Much of the fascination of chess stems from the special end its inventor gave it. It gives chess a unique, mystical quality.

THE BOARD

The board consists of 64 squares. These are called 'black' and 'white', but may be of any two colours. Always place the board so that each player's *right-hand corner square is white*, that is, the lighter colour.

There is no point in having squares the same colours as the pieces. Black and white (or cream) are quite good colours for the pieces, but for the squares a sharp contrast is too dazzling. One of many satisfactory combinations is dark brown and buff.

The rows of squares are called 'lines'. Cross-lines are 'ranks', vertical lines are 'files'. Lines of squares of the same colour are called 'diagonals'.

A natural question for prospective players is, what size should a board be? A good answer is that the squares should each be roughly 1½ times the length of the base diameter of your largest piece, which is always the King. If the squares are a little larger than that, no matter; but if they are substantially smaller, the pieces will be crowded. This looks ugly and makes the game harder.

A small, cheap set is adequate when you start to play chess. For big events, the King is usually 8.5 – 9.5 cm high and the squares about 5.5 cm per side.

'Staunton' pattern is a stylised design, accepted internationally for all tournament play. Plastic Staunton sets, now in general use, are cheaper than wooden ones. Ornamental sets are for decoration.

THE PIECES

Original Position

Each player has eight Pieces, which start on the back rank, posted behind the eight Pawns – see Diagram 1.

Each player has two Rooks (in the corners), two Knights (next to the Rooks), two Bishops (next to the Knights), and in the centre the King and Queen. Note that the **Queen always starts on a square of her own colour**.

Note also that in a diagram the **white Pawns are always moving upward, black downward**.

Take careful note of one ambiguity in talking and writing about chess. The word 'pieces' can be used to denote all the units including the pawns, e.g. in the heading that tops this section, or it can be used for only the major units as distinct from the pawns. It is so used in the first paragraph of the previous page, also in the heading below, and indeed nearly everywhere in this book.

The word piece is often used in a still more limited sense. 'Winning a piece' always means winning a Bishop or Knight. Strictly, these two pieces, which are about equal in value, are called 'minor Pieces', and the Queen and Rooks 'major Pieces', but these expressions are seldom used.

THE PIECES' MOVES

The players move alternately, one unit at a time. White moves first.

The first thing to know about the moves is that no unit, with the single exception of the Knight, can jump over another unit, either friend or foe.

The Rook moves forwards, backwards, or sideways, in one straight line – that is, along rank or file, and as many squares as it likes provided nothing is in its way.

The Bishop moves only along a diagonal, forwards or backwards, and as many squares as it likes provided nothing is in its way.

The Queen combines the powers of Rook and Bishop – that is, moves straight ahead, straight back, sideways, or along a diagonal, and as many squares as it likes provided nothing is in the way.

The King moves in any direction, like the Queen, but only one square at a time.

Thus the King can move to any one of eight squares shown in the diagram. See more about the King, pp. 11–14.

The Knight (symbolising cavalry) does not move in a line, but jumps, always the same distance (two squares in one direction plus one square at right angles) and always to a square of the opposite colour to the square it leaves.

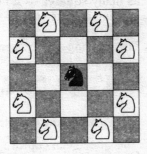

   In the diagram the eight squares available to the central Knight are indicated by white Knights. From a corner, a Knight commands only two squares.

CAPTURING

A Piece can capture an enemy unit standing on any square to which the Piece can legitimately move. It captures by placing itself on the square occupied by the enemy unit; the captured unit is removed from the board. Capture is not compulsory as in draughts.

Diagram 2

Queen takes any Pawn

In Diagram 2 the Queen can capture any of the five Pawns, but not the Pieces standing beyond them, as this would involve jumping over the Pawns.

Diagram 3

Knight takes any Pawn

In Diagram 3 the Knight can take any Pawn; the Pieces in between make no difference, as the Knight's move is a jump.

THE PAWN

We have seen that Pieces move in all directions.
Pawns move only straight ahead, and one square at a
time, except that on its first move each Pawn has the
option of moving either one or two squares. Another
difference is that the Pawn does not capture with its
ordinary move. It captures diagonally forward. Thus

in Diagram 4 the White Pawn cannot take the unit
immediately in front of it – the Bishop – but can take
either of the other units – the Knight or Pawn.

PAWN PROMOTION

On reaching the eighth row a Pawn must take the
rank of any Piece except a King. Naturally a Queen is
the almost invariable choice. This promotion means
a huge increase in force, and is much more important than 'crowning' in draughts. You can make a
Pawn a Queen even though your original Queen is

on the board. This calls for a cotton-reel or an inverted Rook.

Promotion takes effect at once. Thus, in Diagram 5, White can capture the Knight with his Pawn, promote the Pawn to a Queen, and give mate (see pages 11–14) all in one move.

Diagram 5

THE CAPTURE IN PASSING

The capture 'en passant' (in passing) is a stumbling block to learners. In ancient times, a Pawn always moved only one square. The option of moving it two squares forward on its first move was introduced seven centuries ago to speed up the opening.

Now look at Diagram 6a. The White Pawn has not yet moved, and therefore has the option of moving either one or two squares. If it moves one square, obviously the Black Pawn can capture it. But the 'new' rule (about AD 1250), allowing it to move two squares, enabled it to evade capture (see Diagram 6b). In this way it was found possible for the defending player to block up the board with Pawns, facilitating a draw and making a game tedious.

A Medieval Reform

To prevent this, the French chess authorities of the fifteenth century invented a very valuable rule. They permitted the opponent in such a position to capture the White Pawn just as though it had moved only one square. The resulting position is shown in Diagram 6c.

This is called taking 'en passant' (in passing). It is not compulsory, but if Black wishes to do it he must do it on the reply-move. He cannot make another move and take the Pawn later on. Only a Pawn on the 5th rank if White, 4th rank if Black, can take in passing, only a Pawn can be taken, and only when it has used its right to move two squares on its first move.

6a	6b	6c

CHECK AND MATE

When a unit moves to a square from which it threatens the enemy King, that unit is said to give check, and the King is 'in check'. You are not permitted to commit suicide in chess: the King **must** get out of check. It is customary in social chess for the checking player to announce 'Check!', but if he or she omits to do so, the check is 'on' just the same, and the opponent must get out of it.

There are three possible ways of getting out of check:

1 capturing the checking unit
2 moving the King to a square where it is no longer in check
3 interposing something between the King and the checking piece.

Note: the third way is not available against a Knight.

In Diagram 7, Black is in check and has the choice of all three ways of getting out – one a capture, one (and only one) a King move, and one an interposition. (There is only one King move because others would move the King into check from other units.)

Diagram 7

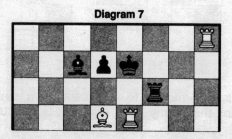

If none of these things can be done, it is 'mate', which the player announces (avoiding a triumphant tone). This ends the game.

In Diagrams 8, 9 and 10 Black is mated. Turn back also to Diagram 5, in which White can mate in one move. Note that in Diagram 10 if the rook were not protected, the King could take it.

Diagram 8

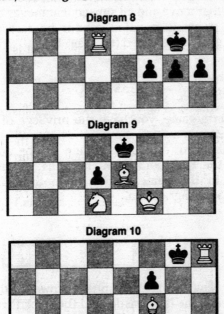

Diagram 9

Diagram 10

Black is 'mated'

If a player makes a move that places his or her King in check the move must be retracted and another made (with the Piece moved if that be legally possible).

As a King can never move into check, it follows that **it can never move to a square next to the enemy King**. If a King is left in check for even one move, that move and all subsequent moves are void. If the previous position cannot be restored, the whole game is replayed (see page 83).

CASTLING

Once in a game, you have the privilege of moving two pieces in a single move – the King and one Rook. This is called 'castling'. Castling can be done only when the **King and Rook have as yet made no move in the game, and have nothing between them**. See Diagram 11a.

Diagram 11a

The King moves two squares towards the Rook with which he is to castle, and the Rook then jumps over the King on the square just beyond him. In Diagram 11b, White has castled with his King's

Diagram 11b

Rook; in Diagram 11c, he has castled with his Queen's Rook.

Diagram 11c

You cannot castle to get out of check; while castling your King must not, of course, move into check; and the King must not even cross a square in range of an enemy piece. But the Rook may cross such a square (this can happen in castling with the Queen's Rook).

A King which has been checked earlier in the game is still free to castle if he has never moved and is not in check when castling is being considered.

Castling: Some Explanation

The purpose of castling is to bring the King away from the centre, where the game is usually opened up, and to bring the Rook to a position where it will not be shut out of play by its own King. Note from Diagrams 11b and 11c that castling with the King's Rook brings the King further from the centre and is therefore usually safer.

Castle early and keep your King sheltered with pawns. When you need to guard against the oft-recurring mate in Diagram 8, move your Rook's pawn (one square only).

Here we add some remarks which the beginner may skip now and study at a second reading. To be prevented from castling is usually a serious handicap because your King is likely to become exposed. But the handicap may be infinitesimal if the Queens have been exchanged off. If at least one pair of Rooks and at least two pairs of minor Pieces (Bishops, Knights) have also been exchanged, having your King uncastled and therefore near the centre is usually an asset (see page 46). So if prevented from castling, seek wholesale exchanges, especially of the Queens.

Castling early, usually advisable, can be a major blunder if your opponent has a great preponderance of pieces on the wing where you think of castling. In such a case, delay castling or consider castling on the other wing.

Alice, now a promoted pawn, with the White Queen and the Red Queen.

Illustration by Tenniel to Lewis Carroll's Through the Looking-Glass and what Alice Found There.

DRAWN GAMES

In competitive play the effect of a draw is that each player scores half a win, i.e. half a point. The latest Laws of Chess recognise only four distinct ways in which a game of chess may be drawn.

1 By agreement.

It used to be permissable to offer a draw at any stage of a game. The introduction of chess clocks, however, made it necessary to forbid a player to distract his or her opponent while the latter's clock was ticking. The Laws now give a precise moment for offering a draw – just after moving and just before starting your opponent's clock.

Even though a player keeps within this rule, if he or she keeps offering a draw repeatedly 'without reasons manifestly well founded', the player can still be accused of worrying the opponent and 'may incur penalties extending even to forfeiture of the game'. In actual practice there is always a warning first.

An offer of a draw may be quite informal, e.g., 'Draw?'. The reply varies from a curt 'No' (a head-shake is more polite) to an equivocal 'Let's play on for a while'. You need make no reply at all. Simply making a move counts as a refusal. You cannot be compelled to talk in chess, except for a single phrase in archaic French (see 'Laws of Chess', page 83).

If both armies are reduced below the strength needed to mate, e.g. King against King, or King and Bishop (or Knight) against King, the players normally agree to a draw automatically. But it is not compulsory. So against an obstinate opponent you might need to invoke method 4, the Fifty-Move Rule. The authors have never seen this lunacy occur in real life.

2 By stalemate.

When a player is not in check as the pieces stand but has no move except one that would place the King in check (see Diagram 12), it is stalemate. It is not mate, because it is not even check. The game cannot go on, as the stalemated player has no legal move, and yet neither player has won. So the game is called a draw. Stalemate adds a touch of quaintness to chess.

Diagram 12

A routine stalemate position is the one shown in Diagram 13. If it is Black's move the game is drawn, because, as in Diagram 12, he has no legal move but is not in check.

Diagram 13

Another common stalemate is seen in Diagram 14. Millions of beginners have carelessly played into it when trying to win with King and Queen against King, which, apart from this stumbling block, is easy (see page 71).

Diagram 14

3 By triple recurrence of position.

Only the player whose turn it is to move can claim

this draw. He must prove that the existing position has occurred **twice before** at his turn to move, or else that by his next move, which he must indicate but not play, he could produce a position that has occurred twice before with his opponent to move.

The draw by recurrence is often called a draw by repetition. Repetition of a position, yes. But many players think it means 'repetition of moves' and actually call it that. They think that moves themselves have to be repeated. But the moves that produce the first, second and third occurrence of a position need not be the same. They are irrelevant. See the *Laws of Chess, Official Code*.

Diagram 15

White to move, draws

A particular case of (3) is Perpetual Check. In Diagram 15, White's Queen could check interminably on white squares.

4 By the fifty-move rule.

When each player has made 50 successive moves

without a capture or pawn move. Rare.

In a competitive game, a player writes down each move as it is played, so a 50-move claim is easily settled.

Above is a drawing of one of the famous Lewis chessmen. These were found in 1831, buried in a sandbank in the Isle of Lewis, the largest island of the Outer Hebrides. Carved of walrus ivory, they may have come from Iceland, and some authorities date them to the twelfth century. There were four sets, not all complete. Most of the pieces are now in the British Museum.

According to legend, they were stolen by a sailor from a ship anchored in Loch Hamnaway, soon after the year 1600. A shepherd known as Ghillie Ruadh murdered the sailor to get the treasure, but, fearing discovery, carefully buried the pieces. A few years later he was hanged in Stornoway for another crime, and is said to have made a dying confession to the murder of the sailor.

VALUES OF THE PIECES

Over 20 per cent of moves in chess are captures. So it is vital to have an idea of the average values of the six different units of force.

Each Piece has an average value. For the Queen, Rook and Bishop, it is closely proportionate to the average number of squares it controls. An unobstructed Rook always controls 14, but a Bishop's range varies from 13 to 7, and averages just under 9. On that basis a Rook is worth at least $1\frac{1}{2}$ Bishops, and in practice this holds.

Similar calculation would rate a Knight as much weaker than a Bishop, but special factors favour the Knight so much that its true average value approximates to a Bishop's. Factors favouring the Knight are it cannot be obstructed, and it has access to all 64 squares, a Bishop only to 32.

In freak positions the average values can be temporarily quite false, but normally they are a good guide. The unit is always taken as an average pawn, i.e., a pawn that has no special advantage, like being 'passed' (see page 25), or part of a mating net.

Average values are:

- minor Piece (Bishop or Knight) equals 3 Pawns ($3\frac{1}{2}$ in early stages)

- Rook equals minor Piece plus $1\frac{1}{2}$ to 2 Pawns
- Queen equals 2 Rooks, or 3 minors; or Rook, minor and $1\frac{1}{2}$ Pawns.
- Summary: minor 3($3\frac{1}{2}$), Rook 5, Queen 9–10.

About Pawns

In the early stages of the game, the Pawns have various functions. Those in the centre, the most valuable, are used for guarding central squares. Pawns in front of a castled King are used as a shelter. To wreck the shelter, the enemy often advances Pawns upon yours, to force them to advance or exchange; this operation is called a pawn-storm. Here the Pawns play the part of tanks rather than infantry.

Pawns sometimes resemble neither tanks nor infantry; their lack of mobility makes them more like natural obstructions (e.g. rivers, hills or marshes) that interfere with mobile warfare. When one of your own Pawns becomes an obstruction to your attack, it often pays to sacrifice it.

A Pawn's value increases as pieces are exchanged off, for when both armies are so reduced that mate becomes next to impossible, the major objective becomes the 'queening' of a pawn (see 'Pawn Promotion' on pages 9–10). This stage, not reached in all games, is called the end-game; it is for many players the most fascinating part. To be a Pawn ahead with otherwise as good a position as your opponent's, is usually a winning advantage, theoretically.

Passed Pawns

When a Pawn has no enemy Pawn that could hinder it from queening – that is, no enemy Pawn in front of it on its own file or either of the next-door files – it is called a Passed Pawn. A Passed Pawn in the end-game is a great asset, particularly if well advanced, as the enemy has to use Pieces to stop it queening, thus reducing their efficiency.

Minor Pieces

Since the Knight can jump over the other pieces, it is good on a crowded board. A Knight 'fork' (see page 41) is a deadly coup.

A well-posted Knight is as good as a well-posted Bishop, but it takes longer for a Knight to get to a good post.

Power of Two Bishops

A Bishop is handicapped by being barred from half the squares of the board, since it moves only on squares of one colour. This handicap disappears if its fellow Bishop is still on the board; with open diagonals a team of two Bishops is particularly strong. Because of this, an early exchange of a Bishop for a Knight is to be avoided unless something is clearly gained.

Value of the Rook

Winning a Rook for a minor Piece (a Bishop or a Knight) is called 'winning the exchange'. 'The exchange' is worth, on the average, nearly two Pawns. Two minor Pieces equal a Rook and two Pawns for most of the way, but (unless they are two Bishops) only a Rook and one Pawn if the other Pieces have been exchanged, when the comparative value of Rooks increases. Rooks like the great open spaces and are therefore strongest in the end-game when the board is comparatively clear of obstruction.

Value of the Queen

Before the end-game, the Queen is worth two Rooks, but in the End-Game the two Rooks are nearly always worth a Pawn more, unless the Rooks' King is exposed to checks.

Another approximate equivalent of a Queen is three minor Pieces, e.g. two Knights and a Bishop are almost always at least equal to a Queen, and two Bishops and a Knight are usually superior. Rook plus Bishop (or Knight) plus two Pawns are almost always superior to a Queen. Exceptions to these valuations occur where the King of the army opposing the Queen is very exposed, so the Queen can organise many checks, giving itself virtually several successive moves while the opponent is powerless to make useful replies.

About the King

Since the fate of the game hangs on the King, it cannot be given a numerical value. However, when so many pieces have been exchanged that mate is no longer a serious danger, **it may and indeed must be used as a fighting piece**. As such it rates well below a Rook but above a Bishop or Knight.

When most of the fighting pieces (i.e. pieces other than Pawns) have been exchanged, including the Queens and at least one pair of Rooks, your King ceases to need shelter of pawns in a corner. Use him as a marauder right in the enemy lines (see second-last paragraph of 'Castling' on page 16).

HOW TO READ MOVES

You cannot read the rest of this book, or make progress at chess, without being able to read chess moves. There are two main notations, Algebraic and Descriptive. Algebraic is easier and used in this book as it is now the compulsory notation used in all international tournaments. Descriptive was used by nearly all chess writers in English until the early eighties.

The authors strongly advise students to familiarise themselves with both: Algebraic in the Abbreviated form for studying modern chess books and for recording their own games; Descriptive for studying chess books published some years ago. Many of these books are classics that should be read and studied by all students.

Algebraic is quicker and more precise, which is a big consideration in competitive play under a time limit. Every move in a competition game must be recorded by each player.

Both notations use the following symbols, except that Algebraic omits P. The omission indicates a pawn move.

K	– King	N	– Knight
Q	– Queen	R	– Rook
B	– Bishop	P	– Pawn

(Kt can also be used for 'Knight'.)

–	moves to
x	takes
+	check (Algebraic)
ch	check (Descriptive)
++	checkmate
0–0	castles (Kingside)
0–0–0	castles (Queenside)
e.p.	en passant (in passing)
!	best move
!!	beautiful move
?	an error
??	bad blunder
!?	may be strong, needs examination
?!	bold but unsound
...	indicates that the following move is made by Black, e.g., 1 ... e7–e5.

ALGEBRAIC NOTATION

Diagram 16 overleaf shows how Algebraic notation works. It is compulsory at all international tournaments and many local chess associations insist on it being used.

The files (vertical lines), from White's left to right, i.e. Black's right to left, are lettered a, b, c, d, e, f, g, h. (Lower case letters are used always.) The obvious drawback is the similarity of c and e in small print.

The ranks (cross rows) are numbered always from White's side, 1 to 8.

Diagram 16

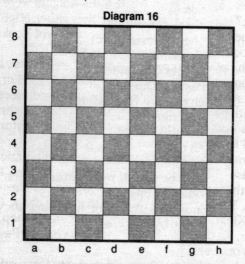

The name of each square is the letter designating the file followed by the number of the rank.

Diagram 21 on page 38 shows the following White pieces: King on f1, Bishop on a4, Pawns (left to right) a2, b2, c2, f2, g2, h2. Black pieces: King on f8, Bishop d6, Pawns a6, b7, c5, f7, g7, h7.

In Algebraic notation the symbol letter of the piece is followed by the square it leaves and the square it moves to. In Abbreviated Algebraic only the destination square is given, except where there could be ambiguity. For instance, if two Knights could go to g6 – one from e5, the other from h4 – the move must be written as either Neg6 or Nhg6. If the Knights were on e5 and e7 the move would be written either N5g6 or N7g6. The same rule applies to the moves of Rooks if either Rook could go to the same square.

In both notations captures are indicated by 'x', but many Continental players use a colon, e.g. g5:f6 or f6: (in Abbreviated). In either case the captured piece is not mentioned. Sometimes in Abbreviated Algebraic the 'x' is omitted, especially when a Pawn captures, e.g. dxe4 is written de4.

Algebraic notation is now used by all nations, which use their own symbols for the pieces. The nearest thing to an international language in chess is German. The German symbols for pieces are K (for *Koenig*, King), D (*Dame*, Queen), L (*Laufer*, Bishop), S (*Springer*, Knight), T (*Turm*, Rook), B (*Bauer*, Pawn) which is omitted.

In books and magazines which cater for readers from different nations, pictorial symbols instead of letters are used.

Russian symbols are easily learnt and can be followed in Algebraic Notation. And Russian books are relatively cheap.

DESCRIPTIVE NOTATION

In Descriptive notation each square has a name, consisting of a letter or letters and a number. The letter stands for the file, and the number for the rank on which the square is situated.

In Descriptive the letter Q or K often precedes B, N or R, indicating that the piece moved is the one that started off on the King's side or the Queen's side – for example, QR for Queen's Rook. This is necessary to avoid ambiguity.

Diagram 17

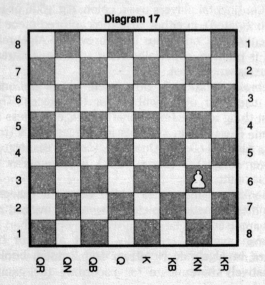

Diagram 17 enables you to name a square instantly. The files are named after the Pieces that occupy them at the beginning of the game, the ranks are numbered 1 to 8, starting from the side of whichever player is moving. In Diagram 17 the ranks are numbered from White's viewpoint on the left, and from Black's on the right. You can see at once that the White Pawn is on KN3, reading from White's side, or KN6 from Black's.

In the practice game (page 58), the first move P–K4 means 'Pawn moves to K4', N–QB3 means 'Knight moves to QB3'.

For a capture 'x' is used, followed by the name of the unit taken – for example, PxQBP means 'Pawn takes Pawn standing on the QB file'.

For brevity, unnecessary letters are omitted. Thus, P–R3 will serve if only one of the Rook's Pawns can move to the third rank. And PxP will suffice if only one pawn-takes-pawn capture is possible.

To assist the student to understand Descriptive notation our practice game (page 58) is given in Descriptive, followed by the same game (without notes) in Algebraic and then in Abbreviated Algebraic, as used by all tournament players when recording their games. Abbreviated is not usually published in columns.

In tournaments every player is provided with a score-sheet in duplicate for recording the game.

When the game is finished each player must record the result on it, e.g. 1–0 (win for White), 0–1 (win for Black), $\frac{1}{2}$–$\frac{1}{2}$ (drawn game), sign both score-sheets and hand in a copy to the Arbiter, sometimes known as D.O.P. (Director of Play).

MOBILITY: COMBINATIONS

A paradox: a Queen is about nine times as valuable as a Pawn, yet an attack by a Pawn is, in general, more dangerous than an attack by a Queen!

Diagram 18

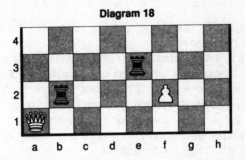

In Diagram 18, one Rook is being attacked by a Pawn, the other by a Queen. The first Rook must move to avoid capture, but the second Rook has the choice of either moving away or enlisting the other Rook's support, by Re3–e2. If both Rooks were attacked by Pawns, one would fall.

In Diagram 19, overleaf, both Rooks are 'protected', but to the Pawn this means nothing, its attack is just as effective as before. The Queen's 'attack', on the contrary, is now quite illusory, for if

Diagram 19

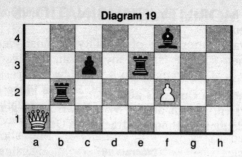

she captured the Rook, she herself would be taken on the next move.

This is a vital element in chess strategy. It means that a larger unit, attacked by a protected smaller unit, must move away if it wishes to save itself. The more valuable the Piece, the warier you must be of exposing it to attack. Your forces are like a fleet; battleships and heavy cruisers must not be unnecessarily exposed to danger.

For example, while several of the opponent's minor Pieces (Bishops and Knights) are still on the board, it is usually a mistake to bring your Queen or Rooks into the open.

MOBILITY IS PARAMOUNT

If an attack by a 'weaker' Piece is the more dangerous, where lies the value of the 'stronger' Pieces? The answer is simply: mobility – that is, freedom of movement.

The vast importance of mobility is most clearly seen when a Piece is, for any reason, deprived of mobility, that is, confined to a very few squares, or, still worse, unable to move at all. Such a Piece is a target for attack, and is often doomed to destruction.

Various ways in which individual units may be destroyed through lack of mobility are now shown. To be able to see such possibilities, for and against in actual play, is the most essential element in chess skill. Coups of these kinds are called *combinations* (see page 64). A sound combination forces an advantage against any defence; it is no mere trap.

The Net

The simplest case is that of a Piece whose lines of retreat are cut off. This Piece may be said to be in a 'net'.

In Diagram 20 we have the common case of a Knight which has captured a Rook in the enemy's

Diagram 20

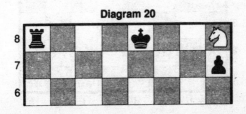

corner. Both the squares commanded by the Knight viz., f7 and g6, are guarded by the enemy, who has only to bring his remaining Rook to bear on the Knight, e.g. by Ke8–e7 to capture it.

Diagram 21 shows a doomed Bishop. This Piece has its retreat cut off not by enemy units, but its own Pawns. Thus –

White	*Black*
1 ...	b7–b5
2 Ba4–b3	c5–c4

and the Bishop falls.

Diagram 21

Had White foreseen this in time, the line of retreat could have been opened by playing c2–c3.

Mate is a 'net'

Mate is a 'net' with the King as victim. In this case the 'net' may be tightened by a sacrifice, often the Queen. Thus, in Diagram 22, White finishes very prettily.

Diagram 22

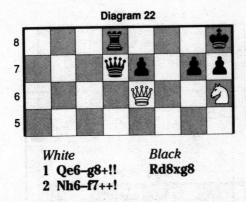

White	Black
1 Qe6–g8+!!	Rd8xg8
2 Nh6–f7++!	

Black was forced to encircle its own King. Remember that a King needs not only shelter but also a little freedom.

The pin

Another way of immobilising is by a 'pin'. In Diagrams 23 and 24 there is a Black Piece unable to move off the threatened line because to do so would put its King in check.

In Diagram 23 the pinning Piece itself will give the death-blow; in Diagram 24 White will play d4–d5 and the executioner will be a Pawn. The Knight is 'protected' by a Pawn, but this does not help it (see page 35).

Note that in Diagram 23, White could take the

Diagram 23

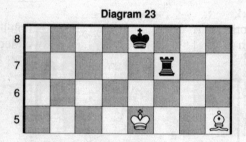

Diagram 24

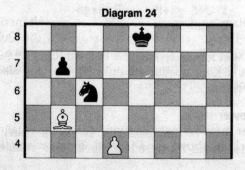

Rook at once and win 'the Exchange' (Rook for minor Piece). But much better is Ke5–e6! first, winning a whole Rook next move.

In Diagram 23, some beginners think that White might equally well play Ke5–f6. This is illegal. A unit (here the Rook) retains its checking power even though completely pinned. Careful thought will show this to be quite logical.

The fork

Yet another way a Piece may fatally lose its mobility is through a 'fork', a simultaneous attack on two Pieces.

Diagram 25

In Diagram 25 the Knight has simultaneously checked the Black King and threatened the Queen; the Queen is deprived of mobility for one move, and is lost. Failure to foresee this possibility in actual play would spell disaster.

The skewer

Another type of combination, sometimes called a 'skewer', is shown in Diagram 26, overleaf. Here

Diagram 26

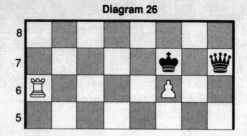

White wins Queen for Rook by checking with the Rook.

TIED PIECE

A piece may also be deprived of its mobility by being tied to some defensive task. In Diagram 27 a Knight is shown tied to the defence of a Rook. White simply attacks the Knight with a Pawn, and either the Knight or the Rook must fall.

Diagram 27

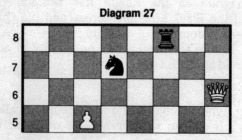

Note that a Knight is the worst Piece for defence, as it cannot move away and still maintain the defence. If a Bishop were defending the Rook in Diagram 27, and a Pawn attacked the Bishop, the Bishop might be able to move to another square on the same diagonal where it could still defend the Rook.

Diagram 28

Diagram 28 shows a subtler example. Here the White Rook is tied to the back rank because if it went away the Black Rook would mate. This gives Black the opportunity for a pretty coup: Qb2–d4. The Rook cannot take the Queen, so the Queen is in effect forking the White Rook and Bishop. Black after ... Qb2–d4 is threatening, then ... Qd4xdl; Ba4xdl Re5–el mate.

Such positions should be avoided by moving a Pawn one square to make an escape for the King, for example by h2–h3.

From these examples remember . . . that using a
Piece for defence is itself a disadvantage.

A Cramped Game

Lack of mobility does not always lead to rapid
disaster, as the enemy may not have the means of
reaping a quick advantage. But it is always dis-
advantageous, as it limits one's possibilities both of
attack and defence.

As a point of higher strategy to be digested at a
second reading, do not, as a rule, attempt to take
advantage of an opponent's cramped position by
attacking it. For the attack may free the enemy.
Rather, concentrate on preserving and increasing
the cramp. Prevent freeing moves. Play the boa
constrictor rather than the tiger. The cramp should
grow to a point where your opponent must create a
fatal weakness or make a desperate sacrifice of
material.

Mobility for Attack

The advantages of superior mobility are limitless. A
small, highly mobile force, by being able to concentrate rapidly in one quarter, may effect mate
against a numerous but scattered and immobile
enemy. Such a position can often be brought about
by sacrificing one or several units to gain time.

Mobility and the Centre

As a general rule, whoever controls the greater share of the centre has the greater mobility. The centre may be said to consist of the 16 most central squares of the board, and especially the four squares in the very centre, viz. e4, d4, e5 and d5.

In the centre, Queens, Bishops and Knights have greater mobility than elsewhere and can move rapidly to either wing as occasion demands.

THREE PHASES

A long game of chess falls into three parts.

1 **Opening** – the armies mobilise and 'mass on the frontier'. During this process, however, 'border incidents' may occur before the main battle begins.

2 **Middle-game** – the war has begun in real earnest. Just as there are different types of warfare, from trench fighting to blitzkrieg, so our middle-game may start by steady manoeuvring for position, or else by the quick opening up of lines by Pawn exchanges, followed by early clashes. The game often finishes in the middle-game through a successful attack on one of the Kings.

3 **End-game** – see page 24. Characteristic strategy of end-game play: the struggle to obtain and finally to queen a passed pawn; the use of the King as a fighting unit.

Let us now deal with the opening, middle-game and end-game in more detail.

THE OPENING: DEVELOPMENT

The object of the opening is to array your army in the position of maximum readiness. This process is called development. To develop a Piece is to bring it into play.

At the start, the Pawns are already 'in play'. None of them is obstructed. It is the Pieces that are obstructed by the Pawns.

Only two Pawns need be moved to free the Pieces: the two centre Pawns, that is the e-Pawn and d-Pawn (King's and Queen's Pawns). The moves of these Pawns (at least one of which should be moved two squares) also help to control some of the important central squares (see 'The Centre', page 51). When you cannot or do not play e2–e4, play c2–c4, for subsequent Rook development (see pages 49–50 and Diagram 30). So, with e2–e4 unplayed, don't block your c2 Pawn by Nb1–c3.

At the same time, observe that the moves of the centre Pawns tend to expose the King. Therefore aim at castling as early as possible (usually on the King's side, as the King is then further from the centre and therefore safer – see 'Castling').

Diagram 29 shows a position in which both sides have developed their Knights, Bishops and Queen, and have castled; their back lines are now clear for the Rooks. This position can be reached by the following eight moves on each side, which constitute a variation of the Giuoco Piano (Quiet Opening). A flaw is that there is no pawn-exchange to open a file for Rooks.

1	e2–e4	e7–e5
2	Ng1–f3	Nb8–c6
3	Bf1–c4	Bf8–c5
4	d2–d3	d7–d6
5	Nb1–c3	Ng8–f6

Diagram 29

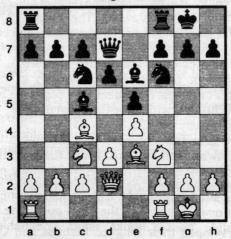

6	Bc1–e3	Bc8–e6
7	0–0	0–0
8	Qd1–d2	Qd8–d7

You have now played up to the position shown in Diagram 29. Here try:

9	Bc4xe6	f7xe6
10	Be3xc5	d6xc5

Black's c-Pawn and e-Pawn are now 'doubled' (two on the same file). Doubled Pawns are weak, especially if 'isolated', like Black's e-Pawns, that is, they cannot be guarded by another Pawn. But here White cannot get at them, and Black has effective files for its Rooks (see below).

Advice on Developing the Rooks

Rooks should be left on the back rank, at the ends of effective files. The most effective files are 'open' files (files free of Pawns); next come openable files (files that can at any time be cleared of Pawns by an exchange); then come semi-open files (files that are clear of Pawns at least half-way along or can be so cleared).

If there are two effective files, place a Rook on each as soon as possible. If there is only one, place at least one Rook on it (if the file is open, one should if possible 'double Rooks' on it, one behind the other). If there are no effective files, as in Diagram 29, defer the development of the Rooks until an effective file is made.

Diagram 30

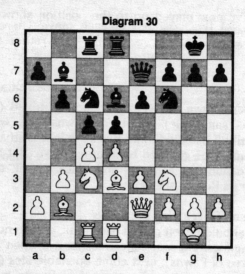

Diagram 30 shows a position of complete 'development' on both sides; there are two openable files as both these files could be cleared of Pawns by exchanges at least half-way along.

Seize any open file with a Rook as soon as possible. But note that the Rook commands the file just as well from the first square in the file as from any other square. Therefore, as a rule, keep it there as long as the board remains crowded. If moved out, it is exposed to attack.

Time factor
Try to get the most out of each move. Therefore prefer to bring fresh force into play rather than move a Piece that is already in play. This principle applies right through the game. The player who completes the development first has the initiative, which is a real advantage.

The centre
The problem of where to put your Pieces when you develop them is solved by the maxim:

CENTRALISE

Let every Piece have some bearing on the centre (see page 45 for important advice).

SAMPLE OPENINGS

Here are two of the most popular ways of opening a game. At each move there is always at least one good alternative, and sometimes a wide choice. It is therefore not important to memorise these lines of play: they are merely illustrative. The important thing is to learn the principles of opening play given in the preceding pages.

Ruy Lopez

White	Black
1 e2–e4	e7–e5
2 Ng1–f3	Nb8–c6
3 Bf1–b5	

This opening is called the Ruy Lopez. A frequent continuation is:

3 ...	a7–a6
4 Bb5–a4	Ng8–f6

Variations from this point are almost unlimited.

Queen's Gambit Declined

White	Black
1 d2–d4	d7–d5
2 c2–c4	

Another example of a Pawn-move with a view to developing the Rooks later on. Compare the Guioco Piano, given on pages 48–9, in which no such provision is made.

2 ...	e7–e6

If 2 ... d5xc4, White can regain the Pawn, the most direct way being Qd1–a4+.

3	Nb1–c3	Ng8–f6
4	Bc1–g5	Bf8–e7
5	e2–e3	0–0
6	Ng1–f3	Nb8–d7
7	Ra1–c1	

The more obvious move, 7 Bf1–d3, can be answered as in the text by 7 ... b7–b6, but a good preliminary is 7 ... d5xc4 to open the long White diagonal first.

Example:

7 Bf1–d3 d5xc4; 8 Bd3xc4 b7–b6; 9 0–0 Bc8–b7; 10 Qd1–e2 Nf6–e4 (forcing a simplifying exchange, usually a good thing for the side with the more cramped position); **11 Bg5xe7 Qd8xe7; 12 Ra1–c1 c7–c5!**

This last is a valuable preparation for developing Black's Rooks (see page 49). Now we proceed after White's 7 Ra1–c1.

7 ...	b7–b6

This enables the Queen's Bishop to develop. The more modern move ... c7–c6 is difficult for a beginner to understand.

8 c4xd5

White does this in order to block the diagonal.

8 ...	e6xd5
9 Bf1–d3	

Another variation is: 9 Qd1–a4 Bc8–b7; 10 Bf1–a6 Bb7xa6; 11 Qa4xa6 c7–c5.

Yet another is 9 Bf1–b5 Bc8–b7; 10 0–0 c7–c6; 11 Bb5–a4 Ra8–c8; 12 Qd1–e2 Nf6–e4.

9 ...	Bc8–b7
10 0–0	c7–c5

This is a key-move for freeing Black's position.

OPENING SYSTEMS

When playing a more experienced opponent you can avoid pitfalls by adopting a 'system' which will assure you of a reasonably good game after five or six moves, irrespective of what your opponent may do.

Against 1 e2–e4

Against the old favourite 1 e2–e4, the authors suggest as the safest answer the French Defence:

1 ... e7–e6 followed by 2 ... d7–d5. It has the advantage that it can be played just as well against any other opening whatsoever. But it is called the French Defence only when White plays e2–e4.

Play over the following illustrative moves.

White	Black
1 e2–e4	e7–e6
2 d2–d4	d7–d5
3 Nb1–c3	d5xe4

Although this move leaves White with the freer game, it avoids many complications. More ambitious is 3 ... Ng8–f6, or 3 ... Bf8–b4.

4 Nc3xe4	Nb8–d7!

Before playing the King's Knight to f6, Black supports it with the other Knight in case White exchanges. Suppose White now plays the natural move.

5 Ng1–f3	Ng8–f6

White must now either exchange, protect, or withdraw the threatened Knight. Withdrawal would interrupt development and give Black a relatively easy game with 6 ... b7–b6 and then ... Bc8–b7. Protection leads to the same position as the text after 6 Bf1–d3 Nf6xe4; 7 Bd3xe4 Nd7–f6; 8 Be4–d3. Then 8 ... c7–c5 as on move 7 below.

Exchange is White's most direct course.

6	Ne4xf6+	Nd7xf6
7	Bf1–d3	c7–c5!

By no means the only move, but the most enter-prising. The following would be one possible sequel.

8	d4xc5	Bf8xc5
9	Bc1–g5	0–0
10	Qd1–e2	Qd8–a5+

This interferes with White's design of castling on the Q-side. If now 11 c2–c3, Bc5–e7 with a safe game.

11	Bg5–d2	Bc5–b4

Safer than the more obvious 11 ... Qa5–b6; 12 0–0 Qb6xb2. Winning a Pawn in the opening often throws one seriously behind in development.

After 11 ... Bc5–b4, Black has a level game. If then 12 c2–c3 Bb4–e7; White is no further forward and Black's Queen can easily move if threatened.

Against Other Openings

As already said, Black may safely play the same first and second moves (1 ... e7–e6 and 2 ... d7–d5) against any opening at all.

If White does not play e2–e4 on the first or second move, Black may safely follow up, on the next three moves, with 3 ... Ng8–f6; 4 ... Bf8–e7; and 5 ... 0–0.

These five moves are not necessarily the best possible in all cases, but they will do until you gain sufficient experience in opening lore.

One example of Black's use of this system has already been given on pages 52–3. After the first five moves, Black followed up with 6 ... Nb8–d7; 7 ... b7–b6 and ... Bc8–b7, and then, to make provision for his Rooks ... c7–c5. This sequence is a good one to adopt generally, provided there is no obvious objection in any particular case.

Playing White

With the White pieces the opening is easier because you are a move ahead. You can obviously avoid special study simply by playing, as White, the same five-move system we have suggested for Black, except that you can always safely begin with 1 d2–d4, instead of 1 e2–e3.

This system makes no attempt to derive any special advantage from the first move, but the important thing for the beginner is rather to avoid falling into traps.

PRACTICE GAME

The following game illustrates several of the principles already given. It is the shortest game in which a master player was ever checkmated, and is first given in Descriptive notation, then Algebraic.

	R. Reti	**Tartakower**
	White	*Black*
	1 P–K4	P–QB3

White's first move is clearly good (see 'The Opening' on page 47). Black's reply, known as the Caro-Kann Defence, violates the principle of rapid development, for it frees only the Queen, and, as we know, the Queen should not aim at developing early. The purpose is to support the move ... P–Q4. If Black plays 1 ... P–Q4 at once (known as the Centre Counter Defence), White plays 2 PxP. Black's Queen, after recapturing the Pawn, would immediately be forced to move again by 3 N–QB3.

Thus we see that 1 ... P–QB3 has a purpose; and, unlike ... P–K3, it does not obstruct a Bishop.

2 P–Q4   P–Q4

Both sides seize as much of the centre as they can, at the same time freeing a Bishop each.

3 N–QB3   PxP

White's third move anticipated Black's reply. In recapturing the Pawn, the Knight will have to move again – an interruption in development. Nearly every opening contains such balancing interruptions on both sides.

4 NxP   N–B3

White's Knight is threatened. The simplest course is to exchange. Instead, White violates a principle by an early move of the Queen. In this case, the error is not serious, but the beginner is advised to avoid such moves altogether.

5 Q–Q3   P–K4

A bold reply, but not very good, for in recapturing the Pawn, Black is forced to make two moves with the Queen, not only delaying development, but exposing the Queen to further attack. Instead, Black should have played to harry White's Queen, by exchanging Knights and then playing the other Knight to KB3, via Q2.

6 PxP   Q–R4 ch

The only way Black can regain the Pawn.

7 B–Q2

Parrying the check with a developing move.

7 ...   QxKP

Diagram 31

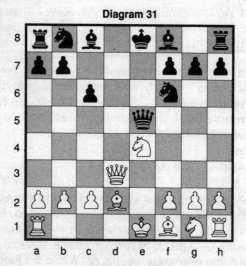

Look at this position (Diagram 31). White needs four more moves to complete development – one with the King's Knight, one with the King's Bishop, castling, and a move with the other Rook. Black needs five. As it is now White's move, White must have gained one clear move since the game began and has a clear initiative.

8 Castles   NxN??

Black takes the offered piece. Black thinks White merely intends to 'pin' the Knight with 9 R–K1. This would regain White the lost piece, but that is all. White has a much better move, with a beautiful sacrifice.

9 Q–Q8ch!!   KxQ

White has given up the Queen for no material return. This must never be done unless you have worked out beforehand that you can force a mate. The same applies to the sacrifice of a clear Rook. But a Bishop or Knight or the equivalent (for example, Rook and Pawn in return for a Knight) is sometimes sacrificed to get a strong attacking position, even when a forced mate is not possible.

10 B–N5ch   K–B2

Note that White's check was a double check, that is, two pieces simultaneously checked the King. In reply to a double check, one obviously cannot interpose or take; one must move the King. Black's only other move is 10 ... K–K1, and then 11 R–Q8 is mate.

Note that if White had played 10 B–KB4 it would also have been check, but only with the Rook. That is known as a discovered check; a double check is a particular case of a discovered check. With 10 B–KB4 ch, White would have got the Black Queen, but only in return for a Rook, after 10 ... Q–Q4 and 11 RxQ PxR.

This, of course, would have been absurd, when White could force mate in two moves instead.

11 B–Q8 mate!

Note that Black's own pieces play a major part in its destruction, as they occupy four of the next-door squares. This factor is present in nearly all mating finishes. Also observe that Black is a Queen and Knight to the good, but is ignominiously defeated, even before the opening is through! This is a lesson to players whose only idea in chess is to grab Pieces and Pawns.

Here is the above game in Algebraic notation.

R. Reti	**Tartakower**
White	*Black*
1 e2–e4	c7–c6
2 d2–d4	d7–d5

3 Nb1–c3	d5xe4
4 Nc3xe4	Ng8–f6
5 Qd1–d3	e7–e5
6 d4xe5	Qd8–a5+
7 Bc1–d2	Qa5xe5
8 0–0–0	Nf6xe4
9 Qd3–d8+!!	Ke8xd8
10 Bd2–g5+	Kd8–c7
11 Bg5–d8++	

Now the Abbreviated Algebraic notation of the same game.

1 e4 c6 2 d4 d5 3 Nc3 dxe 4 Nxe4 Nf6 5 Qd3 e5 6 dxe Qa5+ 7 Bd2 Qxe5 8 0–0–0 Nxe4 9 Qd8+!! Kxd8 10 Bg5+ Kc7 11 Bd8++.

MIDDLE-GAME

With rare exceptions, big advantages are gained only by moves that threaten something, and leave the enemy little or no choice. Operations made up of such forceful moves are called **combinations**. To overlook a sound combination (see page 37) either for you or for the opponent, may be disastrous. So, no matter what plan you have been following, **search for a sound combination at every move**, and make no move without a reconnaissance to see if it would allow the opponent a sound combination.

Combinations are hard to see, as the initial move is often a sacrifice (e.g. Diagram 22 on page 39). To search, look all over the board, thinking of 'nets', 'forks', 'pins' and 'ties' (pages 37–43), and also look at all **captures, checks, and violent threats, even those involving sacrifices**. Usually you will find all such moves unsound, even absurd, but the exceptions will richly reward you.

Usually you have no sound combination, you cannot force the issue. Except in very bad positions, **never play a move you know to be unsound**, that is, one which will only waste time if your opponent sees the trap. For time is valuable (see page 78). Instead, manoeuvre quietly for position. You need an aim, a plan. Choosing **aims is strategy**; choosing **moves for them is tactics**. Your aim should be **one the opponent cannot foil**, so it should be simple, not too ambitious, and should need very few moves – though you may have a long-term plan at the same time, as in war.

WEAKNESS IS THE KEY

What to aim at? Answer: **aim at weaknesses**. The King? Yes, **if weak**; but if it is well protected, as it usually is, an attack in this quarter will fail, and **an attack that fails usually allows a counter-attack that succeeds**. So if the enemy King is safe, look for **weak Pawns and weak squares**.

A **weak square** is one that can never be guarded by a Pawn – e.g., in Diagram 32, overleaf, White's c3, e3, f4, g3 and h3, and all the squares on his first and second ranks. (These last are 'weak' all through a game, as no Pawn ever guards them.)

A **weak Pawn** is a Pawn that is **fixed** on a weak square, or can move only to another weak square – e.g., in Diagram 32 White's weak Pawns are on a2, a3, c2, f3 and h4. The first two form an **isolated doubled Pawn**, a glaring weakness (see page 49).

A weak square is like an enemy town with its railways cut; a weak Pawn is the same town with valuable supplies in it. A weak square in the opponent's half of the board, especially **near the centre or near his King**, is a good one to occupy with a Piece (usually a Knight is best) because it **can never be driven away by a Pawn**; but your Piece should have a Pawn protecting it, as in Diagram 32.

By the way, assuming there are many other Pieces on the board, White's King in Diagram 32 does invite attack; such exposure is usually fatal.

Diagram 32

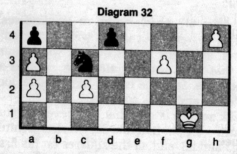

Attack weak Pawns, not expecting to win them, but **to force the enemy to use Pieces for defence**. This reduces his mobility and gives you the initiative – an advantage that can grow like a snowball.

Avoid creating weakness in your own camp unless you gain something in return. Keep your Pawns connected, and **never move a Pawn at all without a clear reason**.

Play aggressively when you can. But you cannot always. Sometimes your aim must be to dislodge or exchange strongly posted enemy Pieces, or to eliminate some weakness of your own.

Above all, never make a move without a simple and clear-cut reason you could explain to anybody. If your idea is vague, it is bad.

In playing over published games, as you should for practice, notice how experts frequently give up material, especially a Pawn, to increase the mobility of their Pieces. Try to copy them in your games and you will gradually learn by experience the real value of mobility as compared with material.

EXCHANGING

With a material advantage **seize every opportunity to reduce the forces by exchanging Pieces (not Pawns) – provided that you do not exchange very well-posted Pieces for badly posted ones.**

You can win by a direct attack in the middle-game only if the opponent gives you the opportunity. Unless that opportunity is presented, you will never win until you have queened a Pawn; this can rarely be done until an end-game is reached, so that the foolishness of trying to avoid exchanges (if you are ahead) is clear.

It seldom pays to evade an exchange by a retreat, except to preserve two Bishops (see page 25).

ANOTHER GAME

Here is a second illustrative game, more briefly annotated than the first. Before looking at each move, spend a few minutes thinking what moves you yourself would consider.

This game was played in the Australian Championship tournament in Sydney in 1945. It gained R.G. Wade, the New Zealander, the prize for the most brilliantly played game. Prizes such as these are almost invariably awarded for spectacular sacrifices of material.

Sicilian Defence

Wade	Shoebridge
White	*Black*
1 e2–e4	c7–c5
2 Ng1–f3	Nb8–c6
3 d2–d4	c5xd4

This was the purpose of Black's first move, to prevent White from getting a strong phalanx of Pawns in the centre.

4 Nf3xd4	Ng8–f6
5 Nb1–c3	d7–d6
6 Bf1–e2	e7–e6

Black has a cramped game, but his position is difficult to get at. He will try to offset White's superiority on the King's flank with an advance on the Queen's flank.

7	0-0	a7-a6
8	Bc1-e3	Bc8-d7
9	f2-f4	Qd8-c7
10	Qd1-e1	b7-b5
11	a2-a3	Nc6-a5
12	Ra1-d1	Ra8-c8
13	Be2-f3	Na5-c4
14	Be3-c1	Nc4xa3

This wins a Pawn. If White takes the Knight he loses his own, Black taking it with the Queen. But Black neglected the development of his King's side and his position will crumble in a few moves before White's well-directed attack.

15	e4-e5!	d6xe5
16	f4xe5	Nf6-g8
17	Bf3-h5	g7-g6
18	Qe1-f2	f7-f5
19	e5xf4 e.p.	Ke8-f7
20	Nc3-e4	g6xh5
21	Qf2-h4	Qc7-e5

White threatened mate by Qh4xh5.

22	Rf1-f5!	Qe5xf5

White's 22nd move was very pretty. If Black's response was 22 ... e6xf5, 23 Qh4xh5 mate.

23	Nd4xf5	e6xf5
24	Qh4xh5+	Kf7–e6
25	Ne4–g5+	Ke6–e5

If 25 ... Ke6xf6, then 26 Qh5–f7+ Kf6–e5; 27 Rd1–d5 mate.

26	Rd1xd7	Bf1–c5+
27	Kg1–f1	Ng8xf6
28	Ng5–f3+	Ke5–e4
29	Qh5–h4+	Nf6–g4
30	Qh4–e7+!	

White's beautiful Queen sacrifice leaves Black with no defence.

30	...	Bc5xe7
31	Rd7–d4++	

THE END-GAME

Contrary to the popular view, it is quite unnecessary – if not useless – to memorise set openings. But certain end-game positions must be known.

King & Queen v. King

The commonest ending in chess is King and Queen against lone King. This almost always arises through one player queening his last Pawn.

The mate with King and Queen is easy. The two Pieces co-operate to drive the King on to the edge, and then mate is easily effected. See Diagram 33 for the position to aim at.

Diagram 33

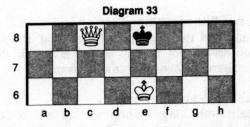

The rule for driving the King to the edge is: **at each step, move whichever Piece is doing least,**

that is, whichever is helping least to confine the enemy King. This rule applies even more to the next three endings discussed.

Once the King is on the edge, great care must be taken not to give stalemate, which concedes the opponent a draw (see page 19). This risk is eliminated by moving the Queen on to the seventh rank as soon as the lone King reaches the edge of the board. The lone King is thus confined until the other King can move into position for the Queen to mate. Stalemate occurs when the Queen and King are both on the sixth rank with the lone King on the edge of the board.

King & Rook v. King

With King and Rook against King – an unusual ending – the procedure is exactly the same as with King and Queen, but a little slower.

King & two Bishops v. King

With King and two Bishops against King, the King must be driven not merely to the edge, but to a corner square, before mate can be given.

King, Bishop & Knight v. King

The mate with King, Bishop and Knight is fairly difficult to bring about in the 50 moves allowed, but the ending is very rare. The King must be driven to a corner square of **the colour on which the Bishop**

moves. This ending is a splendid exercise in applying the important rule on page 71–2.

King & two Knights v. King
A King and two Knights cannot mate against a lone King, without a blunder by the defender.

King & Pawn v. King
King and Pawn against King is the most important ending in chess. From it usually arises the ending, King and Queen against King, already dealt with. It is important to know whether you can queen the Pawn. If you cannot, the ending is a draw. To queen, a Pawn usually needs the King's help, but sometimes it may race through unaided. To tell if the Pawn can queen unaided, count the moves it needs to queen. Then see if the opposing king can reach the queening square in that number of moves. In Diagram 34, overleaf, the Pawn needs five moves; in five moves the Black King will not reach the queening square. So, if the Pawn moves first, it queens.

When each side can force a Pawn through to queen, see which will be first simply by counting up the number of moves each one needs for the purpose.

If the Pawn cannot queen unaided, try to avoid moving the Pawn at all, until you have advanced your King as far as you can in front of it. Your aim should be to take the 'opposition' with your King **in front of your Pawn**.

Diagram 34

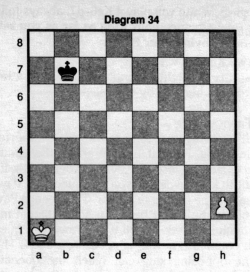

To take the 'opposition' means to place your King on the same file as the enemy King with one square separating them; the enemy King is then forced to move sideways or backwards, allowing your King to move forwards, and make the way safe for the Pawn.

Diagram 35 shows this. If it is Black's move, White has the 'opposition', and wins. If it is White's move, Black can draw.

In Diagram 35, suppose Black plays 1 ... Ke7–d7, White then plays 2 Ke5–f6, if then 2 ... Kd7–e8, play 3 Kf6–e6, again taking the opposition. Suppose then

3 . . . Ke8–f8, White will play 4 Ke6–d7, always follow-ing the rule: **advance your King as far as you safely can before moving your Pawn.**

Diagram 35

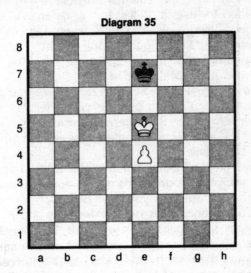

Other rules:
- ■ if you can get your King to the sixth rank in front of your Pawn, it is a win with or without the 'opposition'
- ■ whenever the enemy King can move to the square immediately in front of the Pawn, the game is a draw.

END-GAME HINTS

■ As you have so few Pieces, see that you make the most of each one. For this purpose try to avoid having to use a Piece for a defensive task, especially a Rook. It is only when aggressively posted that a Piece pulls its full weight.

■ Remember that in the end-game the King is a fighting piece. **Make use of it**.

■ A Rook's goal is the seventh rank. Here it attacks Pawns which cannot possibly call other Pawns to their support. A Rook here is particularly strong if at the same time it confines the enemy King to his back rank.

■ If you have a Bishop, whether the enemy has one or not, place your Pawns on the **opposite colour** to that occupied by your own Bishop.

To beginners this rule for Bishops and Pawns sounds silly, because it deprives the Pawns of the Bishop's support. However on opposite colours the Bishop and Pawns together command more squares; they do not overlap. It is the same reason that makes two Bishops so strong.

■ **Always remember**: the Passed Pawn is the soul of the end-game. A Passed Pawn advanced to the sixth or seventh rank is often worth a Piece.

■ With an advantage, keep Pawns on BOTH wings: this helps to avoid a draw. If there are Pawns on one wing only, the advantage of one Pawn extra is, more often than not, insufficient to win.

Hence, Reuben Fine's excellent rule: **for winning, exchange Pieces; for drawing, exchange Pawns**.

THE TIME FACTOR

Re-read the item under this heading on page 51. Apart from positions in which no progress is possible, a player who makes a non-progressive move is said to 'lose a move', or in chess language, 'lose a tempo'.

The loss of a tempo may be of little importance, or it may make all the difference between winning and losing. In other words, a tempo has no constant value.

But it can be given a material value in the opening, because in the opening the general objective is always the same – rapid development of the seven fighting Pieces (omitting the King). At this stage a tempo is usually worth nearly half a Pawn. Knowing this helps you to decide whether to take an offered Pawn.

If you win a Pawn in the opening but lose three tempos (or tempi) in doing so (e.g. by having to move an already developed Piece three times) your opponent's attacking chances should outweigh your small material gain, as a rule.

If you are playing Black, so much the worse, because Black can be reckoned as beginning the game already half a tempo behind because White moves first. If, when the Pawn is offered, White is still his half-tempo ahead, Black will come out $3\frac{1}{2}$ tempi behind.

But if White wins a Pawn at the same cost, White comes out only $2\frac{1}{2}$ tempi behind, and could consider taking the Pawn unless the position is very open i.e. several Pawns have already been exchanged. For in open positions a lead in tempi (development) tells more than in closed ones (very cluttered with Pawns).

An example to illustrate the gain and loss of tempi is the opening: 1 e2–e4 e7–e5; 2 Ng1–f3 Nb8–c6; 3 d2–d4 (known as the Scotch game). Now Black will naturally play 3 ... e5xd4. If White recaptures with 4 Nf3xd4, that also will be a non-developing move because the White Knight was already developed. So neither side loses a tempo.

Alternatively, White may play 4 Bf1–c4, known as the Scotch Gambit (a gambit is a small sacrifice of material, usually a Pawn, for a gain in position). If then Black protects its Pawn with the developing move, 4 ... Bf8–c5, White has yielded a Pawn for a lead of only $1\frac{1}{2}$ tempi. That is not usually a good bargain, but here 5 c2–c3!, while not in itself a developing move, makes sure of opening up the position if Black is to retain its Pawn plus, and experience shows that White's compensation for the Pawn is about enough.

Now suppose White quietly recaptures, 4 Nf3xd4. Here a frequent error is 4 ... Nc6xd4.

An exchange of a developed Piece for a developed Piece always loses a tempo for the player who initiated the swap, if the opponent recaptures with a developing move.

This is easily proved: A has reduced the number of developed Pieces on side by one (since both Pieces end up in the box), and if B recaptures with a developing move the latter is clearly one up.

After 5 Qd1xd4, Black could ingeniously try 5 ... Qd8–f6, hoping White will either move its Queen (non-developing move) or else swap Queens, giving back the tempo by the rule in bold print above. But White need do neither. Simply 6 Bc1–e3 is a developing move. If then Black exchanges Queens, it is true that this time he does not lose a tempo, as White will recapture with an already moved Piece. Indeed, neither side gains a tempo and White stays $1\frac{1}{2}$ tempi ahead. You might think White would gain a tempo with 6 e4–e5, forcing Black's Queen to move again. But no, e4–e5 is not a developing move, since it does not open a line for any undeveloped White Piece, as 1 e2–e4 did.

Zugzwang

Exceptionally, a tempo may have a minus value, for there are end-game positions in which having the move is fatal. This plight is called *zugzwang* (German, meaning move-compulsion). Many end-games feature this motif.

PLANNING

It is much more important to look around than to look ahead. In other words, more games are lost by overlooking the obvious than by failure to see far ahead.

Nevertheless, chess players must always think ahead at least one move. That is, they must never move without first making sure that opponents cannot surprise them with a combination (see pages 37 and 64).

However, a player usually thinks further than one move. After development is completed, and your Pieces are all in play, you should begin to look for a feasible objective.

For example, in some positions you may decide that an attack on your opponent's King is justified. In others, you may decide that such a plan is likely to fail and is therefore bad. But you may find you can win some material, perhaps a Pawn.

More often, you will find it necessary to be less ambitious. Then a good recipe is look for your Piece that is doing least in the position, or one that is doing very little. Then make a plan to activate it. Or look for the enemy Piece that is most effective, or one that is very effective. Then make a plan to reduce its force, either by exchanging it or inducing its retreat. Try both recipes over in your mind.

Whatever plan you adopt, be ever ready to change it. A plan is only something to guide you while the position retains all the characteristics that led you to form the plan in the first place.

Above all, a plan must always take second place to immediate threats – either threats by your opponent or opportunities for strong threats of your own. Threats are the stuff of which combinations are made, and combinations always have precedence over plans. Plans are what you fall back on when there is no sound combination. Admittedly, that happens most of the time.

LAWS OF CHESS

■ Any Piece or Pawn once touched, except accidentally, must be moved (or captured if an enemy) if legally possible.

■ If you wish to adjust something on the board, say 'J'adoube' (I adjust).

■ Once your hand has quitted a piece moved, that move is completed, and cannot be altered.

■ If during a game an illegality is found to have occurred, for instance, King left in check (see pages 11–15), the previous position must be restored and the game resumed from there. If this is impossible, the game is replayed.

■ If an illegality is discovered only after a game has ended (in mate, resignation, or a draw), the game stands. Two beginners might leave both Kings in check for many moves, but if this were not pointed out before the game ended, the result would stand.

An exception to this principle is that if somebody proves that a game did in fact end before the players thought it ended, the moves played after the actual end are null and void.

For example, A apparently defeats B, but the record of the moves then shows that B actually checkmated A at an earlier stage but did not realise it; B must be ruled to have won. Or a stalemate might be proved to have occurred; then the game must be ruled drawn. Or one player might have claimed a draw by triple recurrence (see pages 20–1), and the umpire might have declared the claim invalid. If the record of the moves shows, after the game, that the claim was valid after all, the game must be ruled drawn.

These are only the most important Laws. For competition, you need the full Code, which is readily available.

HOW TO IMPROVE

1 After playing some games, read this book carefully again. Play more games, then read it again,
from page 23 – and even a fourth time! Each time
you will absorb points that were previously obscure
or did not grip you.

2 The way you improve most is not by playing
opponents, but by playing over well-annotated
games. Cover one side's moves (usually the winner's)
and think out each move before looking.

3 If you are eager to improve your play rapidly,
write down the moves of all your games, not only
the competitive ones (in which recording is compulsory). It is best to write them in a chess score-
book, as loose score-sheets are easily lost.
Afterwards, play through each game and jot down
critical comments. One of the authors of this book
used to do this as a boy, and thus became fairly
proficient in a short time without any coaching. It is
surprising how much becomes clear when you
see every position a second time, in the light of
what happened the first time. You become your
own tutor. If, after writing your own comments,
you submit some of your games and your comments
to a competent coach or top player for assessment

for a suitable fee, you will improve more rapidly still.
4 Read chess books.
5 If you can, join a club.

You can enjoy chess without worrying about improvements. But most players have some desire to improve. By following the methods here recommended almost anybody can become a strong player in a fraction of the time normally taken.

Dr Emanual Lasker (World Champion 1894–1921) considered that, given a logical approach, a person of average talent would not need to give chess more than 200 hours to reach a stage where a master player who conceded him or her a handicap would surely lose.

Lasker's '200 hours' was an underestimate, no doubt, but certain it is that most players could reach in months a standard that usually takes them years to attain.

METHOD

High chess skill needs imagination and intuition. But you will develop these qualities all the sooner by thinking methodically, and you will avoid many blunders. Here is the Purdy method. Follow it at every move.

1 *What are the opponent's threats? Or objects?* The threats must be known but, before parrying them, see if they can be ignored.
2 *Have I a sound combination?* See pages 37 and 64.
3 *If not, what should be my aims?* See pages 64 and 81.
4 Before playing any move, consider: *will this allow my opponent a sound combination?* See pages 37–42 and page 64.
5 During your opponent's turn to move: *make a reconnaissance, eyeing quickly all the squares each unit on the board commands. How safe are the Kings? And other Pieces?* See pages 37–42. *What Pawns are weak? What squares?* See pages 65–7.

All of 5 is very easy and wonderfully helpful.

CHESS PROBLEMS

Some newspapers publish regular chess columns in which composed chess problems are a feature. In a problem, an artificial position is set up and a solver is required to find a way to checkmate in a specified number of moves, usually two or three, no matter what replies the defender makes.

For the sake of uniformity, the first (key) move is always made by White.

In two-move problems only the key move is required. In three-move problems the second moves are required for correct solutions.

As the composer's purpose is to make the task difficult, the key move is almost always one that would be unlikely to occur to a player in an actual game, and is never a capture (except of a Pawn) and never a check.

HANDICAP CHESS

The oft-given advice to play against stronger players has two drawbacks. Firstly, it is discouraging if you invariably lose. Secondly, it is painfully boring for the opponent if the difference in skill is great. The stronger player would be too polite to tell you this, but will find some excuse to stop playing. To forestall this, ask the opponent to give you a handicap (give you 'odds' is the chess term), e.g., to remove a Knight, a Rook, a Rook plus Knight, or even the Queen. Once the right odds are found, both players can have exciting games. When removing a Knight or a Rook as a handicap, convention decrees that it shall be the one on the Queen's wing.

Another kind of handicap is possible with the use of chess clocks. The expert can play with a very short time limit, his opponent at a much greater one. If the difference in skill is not too wide, this sort of handicap is better, as there is no alteration of the starting position. If the difference in skill is very great, it is a good idea to use both systems.

For single games, you cannot use a time handicap unless you have chess clocks. But in what are called 'simultaneous exhibitions', a time handicap operates automatically.

Here the expert opposes a large number of players seated in a circle or rectangle, each with a board and pieces in front of him or her. The expert steps from board to board, making a move at each one. Obviously, the expert can take only a fraction of the time that the opponents take, as the master may have to make 10, 20, 30, 40 or more moves in the time that each opponent has for one move.

Simultaneous exhibitions have provided, from time immemorial, an excellent opportunity for a large number of players to oppose a master under conditions that give the amateurs some chance of bringing off a draw or even a win.

DOWN THE AGES

Although it may have had a Chinese ancestor, chess on 64 squares originated in India, perhaps as early as the fourth century AD. Most of the pieces had the same moves as now.

The Persians took up Indian chess with enthusiasm. The caliphs, rulers of the Moslem world, kept chess professionals at court through the ninth and tenth centuries. Chess was brought to Europe by the Moors in Spain before AD 1000.

There was great confusion throughout medieval Europe about the pieces' names. The elephants became archers in Spain, standard-bearers in Italy, couriers in Germany, court jesters in France, and bishops in Portugal, England and Iceland.

The *rukh* (war chariot) was another enigma. In 1527, an Italian poet, Vida, fancifully identified it as an elephant with a tower on its back, as used by Hannibal seventeen centuries earlier. This caught on, but the elephant was costly to carve, and disappeared leaving only the tower – like the grin on the Cheshire Cat.

Europe's first big contribution to chess came about AD 1100 – a chequered board to assist the eye. A century later came the second – speeding the opening by giving Pawns the option of going two squares on the first move.

About 1580 an Italian suggested making the Queen the strongest piece instead of the weakest. Promotion of a Pawn, hitherto a minor incident, became cataclysmic. The average game was halved in length. At the same time, the piece we call a bishop, previously very restricted, was de-limited.

The new game was nicknamed 'Scacchi all rabiosa' (crazy chess) by the Italians, and by the French, 'Echecs de la dame enragée' (chess of the maddened Queen). But it swept Europe like a forest fire, except Russia, where the masses stuck to the old game for over two centuries.

Italy took over from Spain as the leading chess country in the seventeenth century. In the eighteenth century, supremacy passed to France. About 1840, London became the main chess centre. The first international chess tournament was held in London in 1851. It was won by Adolf Anderssen, a German professor of mathematics. Before that, there were matches between leading players of different nations, and to this day the world championship has been decided by such matches, although they are preceded by qualifying tournaments.

The fantastic advance of chess in the twentieth century is best shown by figures. Before 1923 there were rarely more than four international tournaments in a year. Between 1923 and 1939, the average was six. After the Second World War this quad-rupled. In 1974 it jumped to 60, in 1975 to 75, in 1976 to 100. By the end of 1990 the number had increased to well over 1000 registered tournaments!

When founded in 1924, the World Chess Federation, known as F.I.D.E. (Federation Internationale des Echecs) had a dozen member countries. In 1990 it had 127. F.I.D.E. now includes nearly all the countries of Asia and the Americas and many African ones also.

Every two years, a world teams' tourney is held, known as the Chess Olympiad. The number of entries in 1927 was 16. By 1990 it reached 108 teams. Women's Olympiads started in 1957 with 21 teams, increasing to a record 65 in 1990.

The Soviet Union first competed in an Olympiad in 1952 and has won all but two since then. And only for three years since 1948 has there been a non-Soviet world champion. Bobby Fischer (U.S.A.) won crushingly in 1972 but did not defend in 1975 when the title went to Anatoly Karpov by default. Karpov successfully defended his title against the Soviet defector, Viktor Korchnoi, in 1978 and again in 1981.

In 1985 Karpov lost the title to 22-year-old Garry Kasparov in a marathon struggle lasting 72 games, starting in September, 1984. After an amazing 48 games the first match was aborted. A second match was played under the old rules of the best of 24 games, as against the first to win six games. The third and fourth matches between the same contestants were won by Kasparov.

The challenger is found after three years' of elimination tournaments and matches which start with Zonal tournaments, continuing with Interzonals and culminating with Candidates' matches. Women's World Championships are played under similar procedures.

WORLD CHAMPIONS

The title of Chess Champion of the World dates strictly from 1886, but it has been conferred retrospectively from 1866 by general consent. Before that, there were players recognised as supreme in their time. The following list will not be disputed.

1747–95	Andre Danican Philidor (France)
1821–40	Louis Charles Mahe de la Bourdonnais (France)
1843–51	Howard Staunton (England)
1851–58	Adolf Anderssen (Germany)
1958–59	Paul Morphy (U.S.A. – of Irish-Spanish-French descent)
1866–94	William Steinitz (born Austrian, became British, then American)
1894–1921	Dr Emanual Lasker (born German, became British, then American)
1921–27	Jose Raoul Capablanca (Cuba)
1927–35	Dr Alexander Alekhine (born Russian, became French)
1935–37	Dr Max Euwe (Holland)
1937–46	Dr Alexander Alekhine (he died still Champion, and F.I.D.E. then took control)
1948–57	Dr Mikhail Botvinnik (U.S.S.R.)

1957–58	Vassily Smyslov (U.S.S.R.)
1958–60	Dr Mikhail Botvinnik
1960–61	Mikhail Tal (U.S.S.R.)
1961–63	Dr Mikhail Botvinnik
1963–69	Tigran Petrosian (U.S.S.R.)
1969–72	Boris Spassky (U.S.S.R.)
1972–75	Bobby Fischer (U.S.A.)
1975–85	Anatoly Karpov (U.S.S.R.)
1985–93	Garry Kasparov (U.S.S.R.)
1993–	Anatoly Karpov (U.S.S.R.)

WOMEN IN CHESS

In social chess, as opposed to competitive chess, men show no inherent superiority over women. There are many instances of a husband and wife learning chess together, where the wife wins a majority of their games.

Competitive chess is a different story. One basic reason may be that a woman's time tends to be cut into more. But mainly it's fashion and tradition. Young girls generally just don't study chess seriously, as many boys do. The very few who do so have considerable success.

For the past six years world attention has been drawn to the remarkable exploits of three Hungarian sisters, Judit, Zsuzsa and Zsofia Polgar. Judit, at the age of 14, became the world's top-rated woman player, ahead of her older sister, Zsuzsa. The Polgars and a young Swedish woman, Pia Cramling, compete only in men's tournaments, in which they have achieved considerable successes. The Polgars have made an exception by playing in Women's Olympiads, which they won in 1988 and 1990 on count-back from the Soviet team.

Top Soviet women champions nearly all hail from the Republic of Georgia. Two former Soviet World

Woman Champions, Nona Gaprindashvili and Maya Chiburdanidze, were from Georgia and they earned the title of Grandmaster among men, as has Judit Polgar who, at 15, became the youngest ever Grandmaster.

But the fact remains that in the realm of competition the world has open chess and women's chess (although women can always play in open if they wish to) just as it has open tennis and women's tennis.

WOMEN WORLD CHAMPIONS

1927–44	Vera Menchik-Stevenson (Czechoslovakia, became British)
1950–53	Ludmila Rudenko (U.S.S.R.)
1953–56	Elizaveta Bykova (U.S.S.R.)
1956–58	Olga Rubtsova (U.S.S.R.)
1958–62	Elizaveta Bykova
1962–78	Nona Gaprindashvili (U.S.S.R.)
1978–91	Maya Chiburdanidze (U.S.S.R.)
1991–	Xie Jun (China)

From 1950 to 1991 the Women's World title had been held firmly in Soviet hands but in October, 1991, a 20-year-old Chinese girl, Xie Jun, who started her meteoric chess career in Australia at the World Girls' Championship in 1988, defeated the five times champion, Maya Chiburdanidze, 8.5–6.5, in Manila.

BOOKS FOR FURTHER STUDY

Having absorbed the rudiments of the game the reader should acquire a desire for further study. To help the student in this task there is a vast choice of books.

Text books, dealing with all aspects of the game in one volume, vary in scope and price. Some chess manuals are written by champions, others by chess teachers – they all help the beginner to delve deeper into the mysteries of chess. Later the student wishing to improve skills further can specialise by studying various aspects of the game and here there is a vast choice of aids.

Books dealing with openings range from comprehensive manuals in several large volumes, not recommended for beginners, to books designed to explain the reasons why the openings are played in a certain way.

The middle-game is dealt with by explaining the basic strategic principles and by giving examples of tactical combinations. There are many books dealing with this subject.

The end-game is part of the game which should be studied by all aspiring players. Here again there is a choice of many books. Best for the beginners are elementary books which explain basic principles dealing with endings that are most likely to occur in practical play. For advanced players there are books which deal with specific endings in depth.

Finally we come to collections of games of great players. The books with detailed comments are recommended, especially those designed for beginners.

Whilst most booksellers have a choice of chess books, beginners seeking advice should, when possible, see chess specialists or consult their catalogues.

MAGAZINES

The best sources of chess information are chess magazines. Most countries publish monthly magazines, major ones have several.

GENERAL ADVICE

The purpose of this book is to get you interested in chess.

You should start playing, preferably with another beginner, as soon as you have learned the moves. Do not be discouraged if you are slow in remembering the rules. With a little practice you will get accustomed to the moves of the pieces and will be able to start working things out without trying to remember how each one moves and captures.

Chess is competitive and a desire to win is its strongest motivation. This is why you should play with another beginner whom you have a chance of defeating. It is all the better if you have an instructor who can supervise the game to make sure that the rules are observed and to point out where you went wrong *after the game*.

JOIN A CLUB

Don't be shy about visiting a chess club. If you feel timid about playing experienced players you can learn much from watching them play.

If asked to play a game, don't refuse, but you should explain that you are a beginner. Your opponent may be happy to help you by pointing out your mistakes or by offering a handicap.

If you keep losing game after game to more experienced players, don't lose heart. Keep trying.

SCHOOL CHESS

If you are a schoolboy or girl, find out if there is a club in your school. If not, help to start one.

COMPUTER CHESS

It was inevitable in our age of electronics that chess would engage the attention of computer engineers.

The real revolution in computer chess was brought about by the introduction of portable, relatively inexpensive micro-computers. These have been steadily improving and the latest models feature up to sixty-four levels of play, programmed openings and games, a voice announcing moves and sensitised squares to eliminate the need for a keyboard. Most can play a reasonable game, while the more advanced models compete successfully in open tournaments.

Micro-computers are most useful to players who have a problem in finding an opponent. Teaching levels with programmed opening variations and suggested best moves are provided to help students.

For top players computers provide a convenient way of storing information on openings and end-games. Most top players use personal computers for this purpose.